Adventure C

Pirate's Tea Party

WRITTEN BY
WENDY-ANN ENSOR

ILLUSTRATED BY
WENDY LEWIS

Evans Brothers Limited

NOTES TO PARENTS AND TEACHERS

The Adventure Cookery series is intended for use at home or at school. All the recipes have been carefully tested both by my own children and in our classroom kitchen.

Each book begins by introducing the theme and setting of the adventure. There are five recipes in each book linked to the adventure theme and which involve weighing and measuring (both metric and imperial measurements are given). The diagrams and simple step-by-step instructions can be followed by a child, although an adult should always help when the oven is to be used or the cooking involves a gas burner or hotplate.

I have found that if an idea catches a child's imagination an associated activity, such as cooking, can operate as a bridge leading to creative writing, art and craft and the practical application of maths and science. These books will, I hope, help you to provide that bridge.

Wendy-Ann Ensor

Before starting to cook

Remember:

1 Wash your hands and make sure your hair is tied back from your face.

2 Put on an apron.

3 Collect everything you need on the table in front of you.

4 Weigh the exact quantities written in the recipe.

5 If you taste the mixture wash your spoon at once.

6 If you spill anything on the floor wipe it up immediately.

Take care

handles   hot dishes

sharp knives   cooker hotplates

About Pirates

Many years ago pirates sailed the seas, chased ships and stole gold and other valuable things.

There have been many stories written about pirates. Long John Silver was a pirate in a story called "Treasure Island". His left leg had been cut off and he walked with a crutch. He always had a parrot on his shoulder.

Captain Hook was another pirate in a story called "Peter Pan". He had long black curls and an iron hook instead of a right hand. Peter Pan had cut off the hand in a fight and thrown it to a crocodile. The crocodile liked the taste of it so much that he wanted to eat the rest of the Captain. Luckily the crocodile had also swallowed a clock with a loud tick so that the Captain could hear it coming.

PIRATE SHIPS

Long ago, fierce pirates sailed the seas in their ships. You could make some pirate ships to eat.

You will need:

1 good sized potato for each person
1 rasher bacon for each person
25g (1oz) margarine for each person
Salt and pepper
Lettuce
Packet cheese squares
Cocktail sticks

What to do:

1 Scrub the potatoes and dry them. Prick them all over with a fork. Put on a baking tray.

2 Bake for 1½ hours (Reg. 6/ 400°F/200°C) or until they are soft to touch.

3 Cut the rinds from the bacon. Cut the bacon in small pieces and fry over a low heat until cooked.

4 When the potatoes are cooked cut them in half.

5 Scoop out the insides with a spoon into a basin. Take care not to spoil the potato shells. If they are too hot to hold use a clean cloth to hold them.

6 Add the bacon, margarine and a little salt and pepper. Mix well.

7 Put the mixture back in the shells and keep warm.

8 Cut the squares of cheese in half, corner to corner.

9 Make your sail with the triangle of cheese fixed on a cocktail stick.

10 Now place your ships on a sea of lettuce.

PIECES OF EIGHT

Pirates need plenty of food to make them strong. Try these delicious scones and you will feel big and strong.

You will need:

225g (8oz) self-raising flour
25g (1oz) castor sugar
50g (2oz) margarine
50g (2oz) dried fruit
Milk to mix

What to do:

1 Sieve the flour into a bowl.

2 Rub in the margarine until the mixture looks like fine breadcrumbs. Add sugar and dried fruit.

3 Mix to a firm dough with a little milk. Add this carefully, a spoonful at a time.

4 Roll out and cut your shapes.

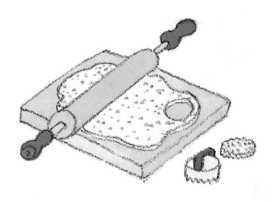

5 Place on a baking tray and cook in a hot oven (Reg. 6/400°F/ 200°C) for 10 minutes.

6 The scones are cooked when they feel quite firm if they are pressed on the side.

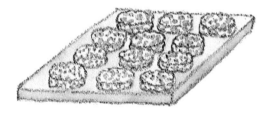

When cold cut the scones in half and spread with butter or margarine. Put them together and arrange on a plate.

TREASURE CHESTS

Pirates used to steal money and valuables which they kept in a strong box with a lid. This Treasure Chest was often buried in a secret place but if you were lucky enough to discover it you might find it to be full of gold pieces or precious jewels.

Now make some Treasure Chests for your tea party.

You will need:

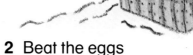

100g (4oz) margarine
100g (4oz) castor sugar
2 eggs
175g (6oz) self-raising flour
25g (1oz) cocoa

What to do:

1 Cream together the margarine and the sugar.

2 Beat the eggs

3 Add the flour and cocoa and mix well.

4 Put into a greased, oblong tin.

5 Bake in a hot oven (Reg. 7/ 425°F/220°C) for 15 minutes.

6 When the cake is cool cut it into oblong shapes.

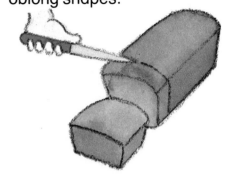

7 Cut the top off each oblong to make the lid.

Icing

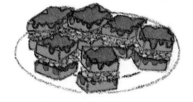

You will need:

100g (4oz) icing sugar
25g (1oz) cocoa
Water to mix
Smarties to decorate

What to do:

1 Put the sugar and cocoa into a basin.

2 Add the water, a little drop at a time, until the icing is soft.

3 Cover your chest and lid with icing.

4 Arrange your Smarties to look like treasure and then put the lid on your chest.

 # CARIBBEAN FRUIT BOWLS

When the West Indies were being terrorised by pirates, these robbers would sail around the Caribbean Sea causing trouble.

On these islands many tropical fruits grow such as oranges, grapefruit, lemons, limes, pineapples and bananas. It was very important for pirates to have plenty of fresh fruit to eat to prevent them becoming ill with scurvy. It is just as important for people to eat fruit to keep healthy.

You could make a Caribbean Fruit Salad using some of these fruits.

You will need:

1 grapefruit for every 2 people
1 orange
1 banana
25g (1oz) castor sugar
1 small tin of pineapple

What to do:

1 Cut the grapefruit in half and scoop the inside into a bowl.

2 Peel the orange and banana.

3 Break the orange into small pieces and slice the banana.

4 Put in the bowl with the grapefruit.

5 Empty the contents of the tin of pineapple into the bowl.

6 Mix the fruit carefully and then pile into the grapefruit shells.

7 If the fruit is not sweet enough for you then sprinkle with a little sugar.

If you eat a little fruit each day you will be strong and healthy.

GROG

Grog is a pirates' drink. It is usually made of rum and water but in this recipe it is made of milk, yogurt and fruit – delicious!

You will need:

600ml (1pt) milk
175g (6oz) raspberries
1 raspberry yogurt

What to do:

1 Mash the raspberries with a fork.

2 Add raspberry yogurt and mix well.

3 Gradually add the milk and whisk well.

This Grog will taste more delicious if you can put it into the refrigerator until you are ready to drink it.

4 Pour into a jug.

Instead of raspberries and raspberry yogurt you could use bananas and banana yogurt.

Activity Page

If you are going to have a pirates' tea-party you will want to dress like a pirate.

You could wear:

a striped jersey or T-shirt

wellington boots

a scarf round your neck

a gold earring
and a black eye patch

Now to make your pirate hat.

What to do:

1 Fold your black paper in half.
Draw your hat shape.

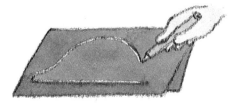

You will need:

firm black paper
white paper
black felt-tip pen
glue
stapler
scissors
pencil

2 Cut around your shape.
You should now have two.

3 Staple the shapes together.
Remember to leave the long,
straight side for your head.

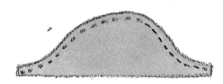

4 Draw a skull and crossbones.
Make the markings with a pen.

5 Cut it out and glue it onto your hat.